THE 'OHANA GRILL COOKBOOK

EASY AND DELICIOUS

HAWAI'I-INSPIRED RECIPES

FROM BBQ CHICKEN

TO KALBI SHORT RIBS

ADRIENNE ROBILLARD
Photos by **DAWN SAKAMOTO PAIVA**

ULYSSES PRESS

Published by:
ULYSSES PRESS
P.O. Box 3440
Berkeley, CA 94703
www.ulyssespress.com

ISBN: 978-1-64604-536-5 (paperback)
ISBN: 978-1-64604-064-3 (hardback)
Library of Congress Control Number: 2020935548

Printed in the United States
10 9 8 7 6 5 4 3 2 1

Acquisitions editor: Casie Vogel
Managing editor: Claire Chun
Project editor: Ashten Evans
Editor: Renee Rutledge
Proofreader: Kathy Kaiser
Front cover design: Rebecca Lown
Cover artwork: kebabs © Dawn Sakamoto Paiva; wood background © Anastasia Panait/shutterstock.com
Interior design and layout: Jake Flaherty
Interior illustrations from shutterstock.com: pages iii, 6, 18, 28, 58, 70, and right page number graphic © berry2046; pages 37 © Kotkoa; page 78 © NataliaKoedit; page 48, 90, and left page number graphic © good_mood; page 84 © EltaMax99; page 93 © Yuliia Khvyshchuk

In loving memory of my grandmother, Dora Gin, who welcomed generations of friends and family to her kitchen, where she generously shared both food and wisdom, and who always made time to listen. I miss calling you on the phone and hearing your cheerful hello! And to my mother, Lily Robillard, who taught me that ketchup is not just for hot dogs.

—Adrienne Robillard

To my husband, Derek, and my mom, Janet, for their boundless patience and helpful advice—not just where this book was concerned, but in life, too. And to my dad, Boyde, for not grumbling too much when I kept stuffing the fridge with piles of grilling ingredients and leftovers.

—Dawn Sakamoto Paiva

CONTENTS

INTRODUCTION

The summer after college graduation, when my boyfriend (now husband) and I were camping at Kahana Bay on Oʻahu's North Shore, I grilled for the first time. It was nothing fancy because we had just enough in our budget for charcoal, matches, cold beer, chips, and hot dogs. We didn't really need much else, except ketchup, my favorite condiment, which we kept chilled in a cooler I borrowed from my dad.

I grew up in Kailua on the windward side of Oʻahu. When I was in the fourth grade my mom won a Nissan Sentra from the local Union '76 station. She'd been filling up the tank to drive to the Job Corps, where she taught business skills when she wasn't carting me and my brother to soccer practices, hula, children's choir, and art lessons. As a single parent, she was often strapped for time and bought ready-to-eat huli huli chicken right off the smoking grill whenever we saw it for sale on the side of the road. She'd put some rice in the rice cooker, steam some broccoli, and we had dinner. Our generous neighbor and lifelong friend planted banana trees in our side yard, and with the existing mountain apples, mangoes, and strawberry guavas that grew there, we always had fresh snacks on hand.

Despite living on the mainland for many years, Hawaiʻi has always been home, the only place I'd ever buy Spam musubi and sushi rolls from 7-Eleven. When my elementary school friend and his wife were looking for a family to rent their house in Kailua, right down the street from my former elementary school and up the street from the house where my mom made mahimahi for us on Friday nights growing up, I took it as a sign. From there a plan to move back fell into place, and I relocated to Hawaiʻi in 2017.

Since that first grill session at Kahana Bay, my husband, Dan, and I have barbecued on a classic Smokey Joe we kept behind our apartment in San Francisco, a series of Weber Go-Anywhere grills we took camping across California, and a number of backyard gas grills. Nowadays we have a larger grocery store budget and more mouths to feed, but we still enjoy the simplicity of grilling hot dogs.

I hope you enjoy the opportunity to experience the taste of island life in your own backyard with this collection of handpicked traditional recipes.

Types of Grills

In Hawai'i we have the good fortune of being able to grill just about any day of the year. Disposable barbecues sold at grocery stores are ideal to take to the beach or park. Shops sell ready-made kebabs strung with beef, chicken, pork, shrimp, vegetables, and fish. I grill primarily with gas, but any of these recipes works on a charcoal grill or your stovetop using a grill pan or skillet, though cook times may vary.

Grilling can simplify meal planning in today's busy world. There are often fewer dishes to clean than with stovetop cooking, and certainly fewer pots and pans in play. There's more time to talk story, to slow down, and to inhale the aroma of the meal you're making. All you have to do is heat and oil a clean grill, cook your food, and enjoy.

Before You Get Started

A clean grill is essential for safety and the best flavor. Locate and check the fat trap and clean it out. If your grill uses aluminum trays in the trap, keep extras on hand so you can replace them as needed.

Preheat the grill to high, allow it to heat for 10 minutes, and then brush the grate clean with a stainless steel brush. Scrape off anything that was left behind from the last use. Then oil the grate by putting some high-heat oil (like canola oil) into a plastic container, absorbing the oil with a folded paper towel—not to the point of saturation, but just enough oil so that it won't drip off the paper towel.

Using a pair of tongs, move the oiled paper towel across the grate. This will help ensure that whatever you're grilling doesn't stick.

Tools and Supplies

Grill tongs are essential for moving food on and off the grill. You should also have a big metal spatula on hand.

Trays made of nonshattering material like melamine are handy for grill prep and serving. I have two and feel like I could really use five.

You need a grill brush to clean and scrape char off the grate. You also need a basting brush for adding marinade during grilling.

Metal skewers are preferable because they don't dry out and catch fire or fall apart on the grill. However, wood or bamboo skewers can work well if you soak them in water for at least 30 minutes prior to use to avoid catching them on fire.

Hot Zones

Every grill is different, and it takes using each one to get to know where the hottest spots on the grate are, how long it will take to cook in those locations, and which areas don't cook very well. The controls vary for different grills. Read the manual for your grill, if you have it, and if not, look it up online. Many grill makers have websites for their products.

Marinating

Marination requires a minimum of 30 minutes but should never be longer than overnight, because the acid that tenderizes the meat can, over a length of time, cause breakdown, resulting in a compromise in texture.

Substitutions

With food allergies on the rise, you may find it necessary to substitute some of the ingredients used in this book. While sesame oil has a distinct flavor, it can always be substituted with vegetable oil. Sesame seeds are always optional. Some shoyu has gluten in it, and some is gluten-free. Check the bottle to be sure. You can skip the fish sauce if necessary.

Pantry

These items are handy to have on hand for the recipes in this book. If I need an ingredient sooner rather than later, I ask at a neighbor's house. We end up talking story for longer than it would take to drive to Kailua Town to shop, but the time spent talking face-to-face is well worth it. How else would I have found out that my neighbor had guavas to share for the making of this book?

- Apple cider vinegar
- Bay leaves
- Black bean sauce
- Black pepper
- Black peppercorns
- Brown sugar
- Calrose rice
- Canned unsweetened coconut milk
- Cayenne pepper
- Chili oil
- Chili powder
- Cornstarch
- Corn syrup
- Curry powder

- Fish sauce
- Five-spice powder
- Furikake
- Garlic (fresh)
- Ginger (fresh)
- Hawaiian sea salt or other large-grain salt
- Hoisin sauce
- Honey
- Garlic powder
- Garlic salt
- Ground ginger
- Ketchup
- Mayonnaise
- Miso
- Mustard powder
- Olive oil
- Oyster sauce
- Paprika
- Pineapple juice (unsweetened)
- Rice vinegar
- Red wine vinegar
- Rice wine (mirin)
- Salt
- Sesame oil
- Sesame seeds
- Shoyu
- Spam
- Sriracha
- Sugar
- White vinegar

Glossary

ADOBO—A Filipino dish and cooking technique known for its strong vinegar flavor, traditionally made with chicken or pork.

BAO—A steamed Chinese-style bun often stuffed with meat or sweet bean paste.

CHAR SIU—A salty-sweet flavor of Cantonese-style barbecue.

CHINESE PARSLEY—What we call cilantro in Hawai'i.

KAMABOKO—Japanese steamed fish cake; the recipes in this book use the basic pink (or red) and white version, which comes either in half-round molded to a wooden board or cylindrical sticks. Okuhara and Amano are popular brands in Hawai'i. Do not substitute imitation crab; the taste and texture are completely different.

KIM CHEE—Kim chee is a traditional Korean dish of fermented vegetables such as Napa cabbage and daikon radish, seasoned with red pepper, garlic, ginger, sugar, salted shrimp paste, and fish sauce, though it can be made friendly to vegetarians by omitting these last two ingredients.

KIM CHEE BASE—Also sold as "kim chee sauce," used to make your own kim chee at home, but also makes a great "secret ingredient" when you want to give things a little more spicy-garlic oomph. Find it in the Asian section of the grocery store (usually with the condiments and sauces, since it doesn't need refrigeration until it's opened, but you might also find it with the premade kim chee) or online.

LI HING MUI—Salted dried plum with a distinctive salty and sweet flavor. The powder is used to flavor sliced apples, gummy bears, and, in this cookbook, grilled pineapple.

MAUI/'EWA SWEET ONION—Sweet onions are grown on Maui and in O'ahu's central farming area and sold in local grocery stores as Maui or 'Ewa sweet onions. On the mainland, Walla Walla or Vidalia can be substituted. These varieties are all much milder than regular white or yellow onions. If sweet onion cannot be found, yellow is recommended over white.

'OHANA—Hawaiian word meaning "family," which extends beyond blood relatives to include friends, neighbors, and those in the community.

'ONO—Hawaiian for "delicious."

PŪLEHU—Hawaiian word meaning "to broil, grill, or roast."

PUPU—Hawaiian word for "appetizers."

SAIMIN—A uniquely Hawai'i noodle soup that borrows from several different cultures; the noodles are versatile and can be incorporated into many dishes. The noodles are sold fresh (uncooked) or frozen (precooked) and usually come with soup base seasoning packets.

SHISO—Called perilla or beefsteak, this plant is in the same family as mint. The leaves come in red or green and are usually about the size of your palm. The green variety can be found in Japanese grocery stores in small bundles of stacked leaves, with the other fresh herbs and greens.

SHOYU—The Japanese word for "soy sauce."

TALK STORY—As defined in *Pidgin to Da Max*, to "talk, gossip, shoot the breeze."

WOK OIL—Intended for high-heat use, there are many brands that offer oils labeled "wok oil" or "stir-fry oil." These have ginger and garlic infused into them and add an 'ono element to your dishes.

WON BOK—Won bok is the Chinese name for Napa cabbage, though it often goes by "Chinese cabbage."

CHICKEN

CURRY CHICKEN BBQ

1 stick salted or unsalted butter, melted

2 tablespoons curry powder

2 tablespoons A.1. Sauce

1 tablespoon dry mustard

1 teaspoon garlic salt

½ cup white vinegar

3 or 4 chicken breasts (1½ to 2 pounds), skinned and halved if they are over ⅓ pound each

❀

Prep time: 10 minutes
Marinate: 30 to 60 minutes
Grill time: 10 to 14 minutes
Serves: 3 to 4 as a main dish
(1 chicken breast per person)

This recipe was created by my sixth-grade drama teacher, Deborah (Debby) Kermode, who taught in Kailua for many years and saw a goofy group of kids through productions of *A Christmas Story* and *The Wizard of Oz*. Debby's Chicken Barbecue appeared in *Island Flavors, Favorite Recipes of the Historic Hawai'i Foundation*. This chicken is delicious on a bed of steamed rice, with the reserved marinade drizzled over it.

1. To make the marinade, melt the butter in a medium glass bowl. Add all of the ingredients except the chicken. Mix well. Reserve ¼ cup of the marinade for basting.

2. Place the chicken into a zip-top bag, pour the marinade over it, and marinate for 30 minutes to 1 hour in the refrigerator.

3. Preheat a clean and oiled grill to medium heat.

4. Grill the chicken for 5 to 7 minutes on each side, turning to cook until done. Larger pieces will take longer to grill. Baste with reserved marinade or use it as sauce to pour over the cooked chicken.

PINEAPPLE CHICKEN

1 (20-ounce) can sliced
pineapple in its own juice
(not heavy syrup)

1 cup barbecue sauce

¼ cup low-sodium shoyu

2 teaspoons sesame oil

2 teaspoons minced fresh garlic

2 teaspoons minced fresh ginger

2 tablespoons olive oil

2 pounds boneless, skinless
chicken breasts and thighs

4 tablespoons chopped
green onions

❀

Prep time: 25 minutes
Marinate: 2 hours
Grill time: 15 minutes
Serves: 4 to 6

This recipe makes use of your favorite barbecue sauce and pineapple, and requires just two hours to marinate, resulting in a tasty sweet, salty, and savory main dish.

1. Remove the pineapple slices from the can and reserve ½ cup of the juice.

2. To make the marinade, combine the barbecue sauce, ½ cup of reserved pineapple juice, shoyu, sesame oil, minced garlic, and minced ginger in a small bowl. Reserve ½ cup of the marinade for later.

3. Brush the pineapple slices on both sides with the olive oil. Set aside.

4. Place the chicken in a gallon-size zip-top bag. Pour the marinade over it and coat evenly. Refrigerate for at least 2 hours.

5. Preheat a clean and oiled grill to medium heat.

6. Remove the chicken from the marinade and place on the grill. Dispose of the used marinade.

7. Grill for 5 to 7 minutes, turn the chicken over, and baste with the ½ cup of reserved marinade. Cook for 2 to 3 minutes, or until cooked through.

8. As the second side of the chicken cooks, grill the pineapple slices for about 2 minutes per side, or until grill marks appear.

9. Remove the chicken and pineapple from the grill, and garnish with chopped green onions.

BBQ PINEAPPLE CHICKEN KEBABS

FOR THE MARINADE

⅓ cup ketchup

⅓ cup low-sodium shoyu

⅓ cup packed brown sugar

¼ cup canned pineapple juice

4 tablespoons olive oil, divided

1 tablespoon rice vinegar

½ teaspoon sesame oil

1 tablespoon minced ginger

4 garlic cloves, minced

salt and freshly ground
black pepper

FOR THE CHICKEN KEBABS

2 pounds skinless chicken
breasts, chopped into
1¼-inch cubes

3 cups fresh cubed
fresh pineapple

1 large red bell pepper,
diced into 1¼-inch pieces

1 large green bell pepper,
diced into 1¼-inch pieces

1 large red onion, diced
into 1¼-inch pieces

salf and pepper

skewers (soak wooden
skewers in warm water for
30 minutes prior to use)

❀

Prep time: 25 minutes
Marinate: 1 hour
Grill time: 10 minutes
Makes: 8 to 10 skewers

Have a pineapple hanging around just asking you to grill it? Based on a recipe from CookingClassy.com, this recipe's light sweetness and subtle tang may easily become your go-to. Include red onions and any colors of bell pepper that you like best or have on hand for a colorful, edible array. It looks as good as it tastes.

1. To make the marinade, whisk together the ketchup, shoyu, brown sugar, pineapple juice, 2 tablespoons of the olive oil, rice vinegar, sesame oil, ginger, and garlic. Season with salt and pepper. Reserve ½ cup of the marinade in the refrigerator.

2. Place the chicken in a gallon-size zip-top bag and pour the marinade over it to coat on all sides. Press the air out of the bag, seal the bag, and refrigerate for 1 hour.

3. Preheat a clean and oiled grill to medium heat.

4. Toss the pineapple, bell peppers, and onion in a large bowl, drizzle the vegetables with the remaining olive oil, and season with salt and pepper.

5. Thread the ingredients onto skewers until all of the chicken has been used.

6. Grill the chicken on oiled grill grates with the grill lid closed for 5 minutes. Then brush it with the reserved marinade.

7. Rotate the chicken, brushing on the remaining marinade, and grill for about 4 minutes longer until done.

MISO CHICKEN THIGHS

This recipe is based on the Miso Chicken from the beloved *Hari Kojima's Local-Style Favorites* cookbook, which can still be found in some used bookstores and libraries on the Islands, with secondhand copies occasionally available online. Kojima cohosted the local TV show *Let's Go Fishing in Hawai'i* from 1981 to 1998 and was host of the show *Hari's Kitchen* from 1996 to 1998. Whether they fished or not, everyone who lived here during those years saw the show.

1. In a large bowl, mix all ingredients except the chicken.

2. Place the chicken into the bowl and coat the chicken well.

3. Marinate, covered, for at least 2 hours in the refrigerator.

4. Preheat a clean and oiled grill to medium-high heat.

5. Remove the chicken from the marinade, place it on the heated grill, and close the lid. Discard the marinade.

6. Cook the chicken for 4 to 6 minutes per side until done.

7. Place the chicken on a platter, and sprinkle with the chopped green onions to serve.

1 (12-ounce) container white miso

2 tablespoons white vinegar

3 tablespoons white sugar

2 tablespoons low-sodium shoyu

½ teaspoon sesame oil

3 to 4 pounds chicken thighs or a combination of wings and thighs

¼ cup chopped green onions, to garnish

❀

Prep time: **20 minutes**
Marinate: **2 hours**
Grill time: **8 to 12 minutes**
Serves: **4**

TERI CHICKEN SKEWERS

1 tablespoon cornstarch

1¼ cups water, divided

2 tablespoons honey

¼ cup shoyu

½ teaspoon ground ginger

¼ cup packed brown sugar

½ teaspoon garlic powder

1½ pounds boneless, skinless chicken breasts, cut into 1-inch pieces

1 tablespoon sesame seeds, to garnish

2 tablespoons chopped green onions, to garnish

skewers (soak wooden skewers in warm water for 30 minutes prior to use)

❀

Prep time: 30 minutes
Marinate: 30 minutes to overnight
Grill time: 6 to 8 minutes
Serves: 4

If you have just an hour to get something 'ono, or delicious, going for dinner, you can make this recipe based on Chicken Teriyaki Kabobs from DamnDelicious.net. Steam some rice and eat these skewers over two scoops, topped with sesame seeds and green onions.

1. To make the marinade, combine the cornstarch and ¼ cup of water in a small bowl. In a saucepan, bring the honey, shoyu, ginger, brown sugar, garlic powder, and the remaining 1 cup of water to a simmer. Stir in the cornstarch mixture until it is thick enough to coat the back of a spoon, about 2 minutes. Cool to room temperature.

2. Place chicken into a gallon-size zip-top bag or large bowl and coat with the marinade. Marinate for at least 30 minutes to overnight in the refrigerator.

3. Preheat a clean and oiled grill to medium-high heat.

4. Thread the chicken onto skewers.

5. Place the skewers onto the grill and cook for 3 to 4 minutes per side.

6. Remove the skewers from the heat. Top with sesame seeds and green onion.

GUAVA CHICKEN

1 cup sugar (if using the
guava concentrate)

1 cup shoyu

¼ cup oyster sauce

2 to 3 cups guava concentrate
OR 2 to 3 cups of Hawaiian
Sun drink concentrate

1 (2-inch-long) slice
fresh ginger, crushed

2 cloves garlic, crushed

6 boneless, skinless
chicken thighs

2 tablespoons cornstarch

½ cup water

❀

Prep time: **45 minutes**
Marinate: **1 hour**
Grill time: **8 to 10 minutes**
Serves: **4**

Guavas are not native to Hawai'i but, since being introduced to the Islands in the 1800s, have become the most common wild fruit here. They can be a welcome find when hiking, grow in many backyards, and add flavor to much of our food and drink. If you don't have access to fresh guava to make a concentrate, ask if your grocer stocks frozen puree or look in the frozen juice concentrate cooler. Hawaiian Sun drinks are one of the beloved beverages that kids and adults here look forward to pulling out of ice-cold coolers at potlucks.

1. To make the marinade, combine the sugar, shoyu, oyster sauce, and guava concentrate until the sugar dissolves. (No sugar is needed if you are using the Hawaiian Sun drink concentrate.) Add the crushed ginger and garlic. Reserve 2 cups of the marinade for later.

2. Place the chicken into a gallon-size zip-top bag. Pour the marinade over the chicken and coat all sides. Marinate for at least 1 hour in the refrigerator.

3. Bring the reserved 2 cups of marinade to a boil, add the cornstarch and water, and mix to desired consistency. The longer you mix, the thicker the glaze will be.

4. Preheat a clean and oiled grill to medium heat.

5. Grill the chicken for 4 to 5 minutes per side, until done.

6. Remove from the heat and drizzle with the glaze.

7. Serve with a side of Classic Mac Salad (page 86).

SHRIMP

CURRY COCONUT SHRIMP

½ cup coconut milk

1 tablespoon curry powder

juice of 1 large lime

2 cloves garlic, diced

2 pounds raw jumbo or colossal
shrimp, peeled except for the
tail and, if desired, deveined

4 cups cubed pineapple,
about 1 whole fruit

skewers
(soak wooden skewers
in warm water for 30
minutes prior to use)

❀

Prep time: **40 minutes**
Marinate: **1 hour**
Grill time: **10 to 14 minutes**
Serves: **4**

I am crazy for curry. Marinating ensures all the curry flavor without the heaviness of a thick sauce burying the shrimp. This recipe also stems from modern master Mark Bittman's Coconut-Rum Shrimp and Pineapple Skewers, found in *How to Grill Everything*.

1. In a large bowl, combine the coconut milk, curry powder, lime juice, and garlic to make the marinade.

2. Add the shrimp and coat. Cover the bowl and marinate for about an hour in the refrigerator.

3. Preheat a clean and oiled gas grill to medium-high heat.

4. Remove the shrimp from the marinade, and place it on skewers alternately with the cubed pineapple.

5. Place the skewers on the grill directly over the fire. Close the lid and cook for about 5 minutes per side.

"IT'S ALL ABOUT THE SAUCE" SHRIMP

1½ pounds large or jumbo shrimp, shelled, with tail on

1 (13.5- to 15-ounce) can unsweetened coconut milk

¾ teaspoon paprika

1 tablespoon minced fresh garlic

zest of 1 lime (save the lime to use for the sauce)

1 serrano or jalapeño chili pepper, diced

⅓ cup vegetable oil

salt and pepper, as needed

skewers
(soak wooden skewers in warm water for 30 minutes prior to use)

❀

Prep time: 15 minutes, longer if you need to shell the shrimp
Marinate: 4 hours to overnight
Grill time: 3 to 4 minutes, or until shrimp are opaque
Serves: 4 as an entrée or more as pupus

Whether you make these as a main dish or as pupus, what we call appetizers, they really are all about the sauce, but prep the shrimp first. While you wait for the grill to heat up, make the dipping sauce. It comes out best if you use a red cooking wine often found in the same area of the grocery store as salad dressings and barbecue sauce. However, you can use cooking sherry in a pinch. This recipe is inspired by Gwen McKee and Barbara Moseley's *Best of the Best from Hawai'i Cookbook*.

1. Place the shrimp into a gallon-size zip-top bag.

2. Shake the can of coconut milk and pour it into a large glass or ceramic bowl. Add the paprika, garlic, lime zest, and chili and whisk together.

3. Pour the marinade over the shrimp in the zip-top bag until it is well coated. Marinate for 4 hours to overnight in the refrigerator.

4. Preheat a clean and oiled grill to medium heat.

5. Remove the shrimp from the marinade. Season it with salt and pepper as desired, and toss it lightly in the vegetable oil. Thread the skewers with shrimp. Lay the skewers on the grill with enough space to easily lift them with tongs. Close the grill lid.

6. Grill the shrimp for 1½ to 2 minutes on both sides, keeping a close eye so the shrimp is not overdone. Shrimp will appear pink when cooked. Serve either on or off the skewers, with 'Ono Dipping Sauce.

'ONO DIPPING SAUCE

1. Heat the red cooking wine and sugar in a medium saucepan. When the mixture comes to a boil, lower the heat, stirring until it develops a syrupy consistency. Allow the mixture to cool.

2. In a blender, combine the mango and lime juice. Add the red wine and sugar mixture and blend. Remove the sauce from the blender and stir in the diced peppers.

1 cup red cooking wine

½ cup sugar

½ to 1 fresh ripe mango, pureed, or 1 cup frozen mango

juice of 1 lime

½ red bell pepper, diced

½ green bell pepper, diced

FOIL-PACKET SHRIMP

3 tablespoons minced
fresh garlic

1 teaspoon chopped fresh ginger

¼ cup white wine

¼ cup unsalted butter, softened

2 tablespoons chopped
fresh Italian parsley

salt and pepper, to taste

fresh lemon juice, to taste

1 pound raw shrimp
(16 to 20 count size), shelled,
deveined, and butterflied

fresh lemon wedges, to serve

❀

Prep time: 15 minutes
Marinate: 1 hour
Grill time: 5 to 10 minutes
Serves: 2 as a main, 4 as a side

This recipe is inspired by Russel Siu's Ti Leaf Shrimp, published in *The Hawai'i Tailgate Cookbook*. Butterfly and devein the shrimp so they curl slightly as they cook and you start to smell that perfect blend of garlic and butter and spice. If you don't have ti leaves growing in your backyard (or your neighbor's!), you can substitute banana leaves or just use the foil.

1. In a large glass or other nonreactive bowl, combine all of the ingredients except for the shrimp. Add the shrimp and cover. Marinate for 1 hour in the refrigerator.

2. Preheat a clean and oiled grill to medium heat. On a tray or cookie sheet, lay a long sheet of aluminum foil horizontally. It's better to make this bigger rather than smaller.

3. Lay 2 clean ti leaves vertically on the foil. Trim off the rigid spine and stem so the leaves can bend easily. If you don't have access to leaves, just make the foil packet.

4. Place the shrimp on the leaves.

5. Pour the remaining marinade from the bowl over the shrimp.

6. Fold the leaves from the bottom and top and then from the sides, making a snug packet.

7. Place the packets on the grill for 5 to 10 minutes. When the shrimp is pink, it's ready. Do not overcook.

8. Serve with optional lemon wedges.

SPICY MISO SHRIMP

Mark Bittman is known for his How to Cook Everything books and *How to Grill Everything* is no exception. This recipe is inspired by his Butterflied Shrimp with Spicy Miso Glaze. Don't try it with anything smaller than jumbo shrimp. You'll want to use miso on everything after making this. You can. Some of the shrimp will char and blacken, making a dramatic contrast with the pink meat.

½ cup mirin

1 tablespoon sriracha

½ cup white or red miso

2 pounds raw jumbo or colossal shrimp, peeled except for the tail, deveined, and butterflied

2 tablespoons chopped scallions, to garnish

❀

Prep time: 25 minutes
Grill time: 4 to 10 minutes
Serves: 4

1. Preheat a clean and oiled grill to medium. Whisk the mirin, sriracha, and miso together in a small bowl until combined.

2. Lay the shrimp out in a single layer on a rimmed baking sheet.

3. Brush the shrimp with the glaze on both sides.

4. Place the shrimp one by one on the grill directly over the heat. Flatten with tongs.

5. Close the lid and grill the shrimp for 2 to 5 minutes on each side. Check for when the glaze has darkened or there is char.

6. Remove from the grill and garnish with scallions.

GRILLED GARLIC SHRIMP

O'ahu's North Shore is famous for its garlic shrimp trucks, where the shrimp are sautéed and then often served with scoops of rice and macaroni salad. This recipe offers a grilling twist. You can use shrimp with the heads on or off, veins in or out, and make it spicy or mild depending on who's eating. My mom is pepper averse, but everyone loves garlic.

1. Preheat a clean and oiled grill to medium-high heat.

2. Place the shrimp in a medium bowl. In another small bowl, mix the garlic, oil, and, if desired, chili flakes.

3. Pour the mixture over the shrimp and toss to coat. Sprinkle with the salt.

4. Arrange the shrimp on skewers, piercing them near the tail and through the top of the body, so the shrimp is curled in a C.

5. Grill, covered, over medium to low heat for 1 to 2 minutes on each side or until the shrimp turn pink. The tails may get charred, which is just fine. Smaller shrimp will take less time. If in doubt, remove the skewers from the grill on the early side to keep the shrimp tender.

6. Slide the shrimp off the skewers, squeeze fresh lemon over them to taste, and enjoy.

2 pounds raw shrimp, peeled except for the tail and, if desired, deveined

3 teaspoons minced fresh garlic

½ cup olive oil

½ teaspoon red chili flakes/ crushed red pepper (optional)

1 teaspoon Hawaiian sea salt or other large-grain salt

fresh lemon, cut into wedges (optional)

skewers (soak wooden skewers in warm water for 30 minutes prior to use)

❀

Prep time: **15 minutes**
Grill time: **2 to 5 minutes**
Serves: **4**

FISH

SEARED 'AHI

4 (½-pound) sushi-grade 'ahi fillets

½ cup shoyu

2 tablespoons honey

2 teaspoons toasted sesame seeds

2 teaspoons minced fresh garlic

3 tablespoons olive oil

salt and pepper, to taste

2 tablespoons chopped green onions

✿

Prep time: 5 minutes
Grill time: 5 minutes
Serves: 4

The quality of 'ahi is paramount. Ask your butcher for sushi-grade 'ahi. You don't want to cook the fish all the way through. It should be rare inside and just cooked on the outside, so when you cut into it you see the bright red fish.

1. Preheat a clean and oiled grill to medium heat.

2. To make the sauce, whisk together all of the ingredients except for the 'ahi, olive oil, and green onions in a medium bowl.

3. Rub the 'ahi with olive oil, and lightly season with salt and pepper.

4. Place the 'ahi on the grill. Sear each side for 2 to 2½ minutes.

5. Remove the fish from the heat. Drizzle it with sauce and garnish with green onions to serve.

GRILLED MAHIMAHI

2 tablespoons lime juice

⅓ cup olive oil

3 tablespoons fresh chopped Chinese parsley

½ teaspoon pepper

4 (8-ounce) mahimahi fillets

SPICY SAUCE

¼ cup rice vinegar

1 teaspoon grated ginger

¼ cup shoyu

2 teaspoons Dijon mustard

¼ cup sesame oil

¼ cup peanut oil

1 to 2 teaspoons hot chili oil (optional)

1 tablespoon sesame seeds, toasted

❀

Prep time: 10 minutes
Marinate: 1 to 2 hours
Grill time: 6 to 8 minutes
Serves: 4

Mahimahi has a reliable sturdiness that keeps it together on the grill. It's what my mom made for dinner on "special nights." This recipe is adapted from Grilled Mahimahi with Sesame Shoyu in the *Let's Go Fishing Cookbook* by Ben Wong, which can still be found at local libraries and, occasionally, in used bookstores or online. If you have sesame seeds that aren't toasted, heat a small frying pan (not nonstick) with a single layer of sesame seeds on it, turning them over once. The sauce in this recipe can be customized to your liking: add 1 teaspoon of chili oil to the sauce for mild heat, 2 for more, or skip it altogether.

1. To make the marinade, whisk together the lime juice, olive oil, Chinese parsley, and pepper in a medium bowl.

2. Place the fish filets into a zip-top bag. Pour the marinade over the fish, coating it on all sides. Marinate in the refrigerator for 1 to 2 hours.

3. While the fish marinates, use a food processor or blender to make the Spicy Sauce. Blend the rice vinegar, ginger, shoyu, and mustard, about 10 seconds. Add the sesame oil, peanut oil, and hot chili oil, if using. Transfer the sauce to a medium bowl and mix in the toasted sesame seeds.

4. Preheat a clean and oiled grill to medium-high heat.

5. Cook each fillet for 3 to 4 minutes on each side with the lid down.

6. Remove the fish from the heat and serve with the Spicy Sauce.

THE 'OHANA GRILL COOKBOOK

SWEET AND SOUR SALMON

4 (½-pound) salmon
steaks or fillets

1 (6-ounce) can unsweetened
pineapple juice

1 tablespoon low-sodium shoyu

½ to 1 teaspoon hot pepper oil

1 tablespoon vegetable oil

2 cloves garlic, minced

½ cup onion, finely chopped

1 tablespoon grated fresh ginger

½ teaspoon lime zest

2 tablespoons fresh lime juice

2 tablespoons fresh
chopped Chinese parsley
leaves, to garnish

❀

Prep time: 10 minutes
Marinate: 4+ hours
Grill time: 10 to 14 minutes
Serves: 4

Adapted from the Grilled Salmon Oriental recipe in the *More Favorite Recipes* cookbook published by the Haʻaheo School in Hilo, Hawaiʻi, this recipe offers a fresh take on grilled salmon. Plan on a half pound of salmon per person. Ask your butcher to cut the fish into single serving pieces.

1. Place the fish into a rectangular nonaluminum baking dish.

2. Combine all of the remaining ingredients except for the parsley leaves in a small bowl to create a marinade.

3. Pour the marinade over the fish, turning the fish to coat it evenly.

4. Cover and refrigerate for a minimum of 4 hours.

5. Preheat a clean and oiled grill to medium heat.

6. Place the salmon on the grill and close the lid.

7. After 5 to 7 minutes, turn the salmon over and grill for another 5 to 7 minutes. The fish is ready when it flakes easily with a fork.

8. Remove the salmon from the heat and garnish with Chinese parsley to serve.

SOY GINGER SALMON

Maple syrup is not just for breakfast. While salmon is not a fish native to Hawai'i, it's readily available. This marinade is light enough to not weigh down the salmon while adding excellent flavor. My husband has been throwing this on the grill for years. Serve it over steamed rice and, if you like, sprinkle it on some sesame seeds and furikake, which I like to put on almost everything. Plan on a ½-pound fillet for each serving. Ask your butcher to cut the fish into pieces.

¼ cup reduced-sodium shoyu

¼ cup maple syrup

3 tablespoons olive oil

2 teaspoons minced fresh garlic

1 teaspoon minced fresh ginger

4 (½-pound) salmon fillets

Prep time: **15 minutes**
Marinate: **1 hour to overnight**
Grill time: **15 to 20 minutes**
Serves: **4**

1. To make the marinade, in a medium bowl, mix the shoyu, maple syrup, olive oil, garlic, and ginger with a whisk to emulsify. Reserve ¼ cup of marinade in the refrigerator for use during grilling.

2. Place the salmon into a zip-top bag or container and pour the marinade over it. Chill in the refrigerator for a minimum of 1 hour. Overnight is ideal for locking in flavor.

3. Preheat a clean and oiled grill to medium-high heat.

4. Place the salmon fillets skin-side down on the grate.

5. Grill for about 9 minutes on each side, basting with the reserved marinade as desired.

LEMONGRASS SWORDFISH

2 tablespoons vegetable oil

1 tablespoon sesame oil

2 tablespoons shoyu

1 tablespoon finely chopped
lemongrass with tough
outer layer removed

4 (4-ounce) swordfish steaks

1 tablespoon toasted
sesame seeds, to garnish

❀

Prep time: 5 minutes
Marinate: 30 minutes
Grill time: 6 to 8 minutes
Serves: 4

This recipe, adapted from *Mother Earth Living,* works both as a delicious stand-alone entrée and also as the filling for fish tacos.

1. To make the marinade, whisk together the vegetable oil, sesame oil, shoyu, and lemongrass.

2. Place the fish into a glass dish or zip-top bag and rub the marinade onto it, covering it on both sides.

3. Marinate in the refrigerator for 30 minutes.

4. Preheat a clean and oiled grill to medium heat.

5. Remove the swordfish from the marinade and place it on the hot grill. Cook it for 3 to 4 minutes per side.

6. Remove the fish from the heat and top it with sesame seeds to serve.

VEGETABLES AND TOFU

GRILLED TOFU AND VEGGIES

1 (15-ounce) package
extra-firm tofu

½ cup hoisin sauce

2 cloves garlic, minced

1 tablespoon plus 1 teaspoon
vegetable oil, divided

1 tablespoon grated ginger

1 tablespoon seasoned
rice vinegar

1 tablespoon low-sodium shoyu

⅛ teaspoon cayenne pepper

1 medium to large zucchini,
cut lengthwise into
4 slabs then halved

1 large red bell pepper,
quartered and deseeded

1 bunch green onions,
ends trimmed

❀

Prep time: 25 minutes
Grill time: 10 to 11 minutes
Serves: 2 to 3 as a side

Based on Hoisin-Ginger-Glazed Tofu and Veggies in the *Good Housekeeping Ultimate Grilling Cookbook*, this dish delivers in flavor and quantity, appealing to vegetarians and meat eaters alike. It's essential to use extra-firm tofu for grilling to avoid it falling apart on the grate. Zucchini and bell pepper are terrific for grilling because they retain their structure, but you can substitute other vegetables to suit your taste.

1. Preheat a clean and oiled grill to medium heat.

2. Remove the tofu from the packaging and lay it on paper towels to drain the moisture. Fold the paper towels over the tofu and press down softly to absorb excess moisture.

3. Place the longest side of the tofu facedown on a plate. Cut the tofu horizontally into 4 pieces, and then cut from top to bottom in half to create 8 equal slices.

4. Whisk together the hoisin sauce, garlic, the tablespoon of vegetable oil, ginger, rice vinegar, shoyu, and cayenne until well blended. Place ¼ cup of the glaze aside to use while grilling.

5. Brush both sides of the tofu with the glaze.

6. Gently toss the zucchini and bell pepper in a medium bowl, coating them with the glaze.

7. Rub the green onions with the teaspoon of vegetable oil.

8. Grill the tofu, zucchini, and bell peppers for about 5 minutes total, turning them as needed.

9. Transfer the tofu to a covered platter to keep warm.

10. Continue cooking the vegetables, transferring pieces to the platter with the tofu when done, about 5 minutes more or until tender and brown.

11. Grill the green onions and lay them atop the tofu and veggies.

SESAME EGGPLANT

2 tablespoons sea salt,
plus extra for sprinkling

1 cup warm water plus
5 cups cold water

2 to 3 medium eggplants,
cut into ½-inch-thick
slices, stems removed

⅓ cup olive oil

2 teaspoons sesame seeds

❀

Prep time: 40 minutes
Marinate: 30 to 60 minutes
Grill time: 6 to 10 minutes
Serves: 4 as a side

Note: If desired, use toasted sesame seeds for garnish. Toast the sesame seeds in a clean frying pan on the stovetop over medium heat, and turn them until both sides are golden brown.

The purple hues of eggplant are hard to resist at the farmers market. In some locations they are easy to grow in your backyard garden. For this recipe, you can use the longer Japanese or Chinese eggplant, slicing it vertically, or the rounder Italian eggplant cut horizontally into circular slices. Keep the skin on to retain the shape of the vegetable while grilling. It can always be removed after the eggplant comes off the grill.

1. Dissolve 2 tablespoons of salt in a cup of warm water in a large bowl with enough space to accommodate the sliced eggplant.

2. Add 5 cups of cold water to the saltwater, creating a brine. Brining eggplant creates a crispier outside and robust flavor.

3. Place an upside-down plate or bowl on top of the eggplant to submerge it. Soak for 30 minutes to 1 hour, weighted if needed (a can of food on top of the plate works great).

4. Preheat a clean and oiled grill to medium-high heat.

5. Remove the eggplant from the brine and pat it dry with a clean towel. Place the slices of eggplant on a baking sheet or long tray. Brush both sides with olive oil and sprinkle with salt.

6. Place the slices oiled-side-down on the grill. Close the lid and cook until grill marks appear, 3 to 5 minutes on each side.

7. Remove from the heat and sprinkle with sesame seeds.

GRILLED SHISHITO PEPPERS

2 tablespoons sesame oil

¾ teaspoon grated fresh garlic

½ teaspoon finely
grated fresh ginger

1 tablespoon shoyu

½ pound shishito peppers

1 teaspoon Hawaiian sea salt
or other large-grain salt

❀

Prep time: 5 minutes
Marinate: 15 to 20 minutes
Grill time: 6 to 10 minutes
Serves: 4 as a side

Based on a recipe from The Spruce Eats website, this appetizer is fun to play roulette with. One in ten will be a scorcher. You'll know when someone bites into a fiery one.

1. Preheat a clean and oiled grill to medium heat.

2. Combine the oil, garlic, ginger, and shoyu in a large bowl. Add the shishito peppers and toss to coat.

3. Marinate the peppers for 15 to 20 minutes, turning them occasionally.

4. Remove the peppers from the marinade. Place them directly onto the grill and close the lid.

5. Grill the peppers for 3 to 5 minutes per side. Stay near the grill and turn the peppers with tongs when they blister.

6. Return the peppers to the bowl. Sprinkle with Hawaiian sea salt to taste.

CRISPY CARROTS WITH HAWAIIAN SEA SALT

2 pounds carrots, peeled

3 tablespoons olive oil

Hawaiian sea salt or other large-grain salt, to taste

pepper, to taste

❀

Prep time: **10 minutes**
Grill time: **10 minutes**
Serves: **4 to 6 as a side**

This is one that you don't need to marinate overnight. The bright orange goes great as a side with just about anything: fish, pork, beef, or chicken.

1. Preheat a clean and oiled grill to medium heat.

2. Place the carrots in a baking dish and coat them with olive oil. Sprinkle to taste with Hawaiian sea salt or another salt with large crystals. Add pepper, to taste.

3. Place the carrots on the grill for a total of 10 minutes, turning them as needed when grill marks appear.

4. Add extra salt or pepper as desired.

GRILLED CORN WITH CREAMY KIM CHEE SPREAD

4 ears of corn,
husks on (optional)

¼ cup vegetable oil

salt, to taste

❀

Prep time: 15 minutes
Grill time: 8 to 10 minutes
Serves: 4

Corn grows here and can be seen in home gardens, at the farmers market, and in the grocery store produce section. Instead of topping this crunchy side with butter, give your crisp sweet corn a little spice with this creamy kim chee spread.

1. Preheat a clean and oiled grill to medium heat.

2. Roll the corn cobs in vegetable oil and sprinkle them with salt.

3. Place the corn cobs on the grill. Close the lid and grill for 4 to 5 minutes on each side.

4. Remove from heat and serve with Creamy Kim Chee Spread.

CREAMY KIM CHEE SPREAD

This is a versatile spread that can be used just about anywhere you'd use mayonnaise—even better, you can eat it just like a dip! We put it on hot dogs and corn, but you could also toss vegetables in it before grilling or mix it into pasta or mashed potatoes—the sky's the limit.

½ cup kim chee

1 tablespoon kim chee liquid
(straight out of the kim chee jar)

2 tablespoons kim chee
base, divided

8 ounces whipped
cream cheese

1. Roughly chop the kim chee. In a blender, combine the kim chee, kim chee liquid, and 1 tablespoon of kim chee base. Blend until liquefied. (You might have some chunkier bits of kim chee hanging around—that's OK.)

2. Add the whipped cream cheese and remaining tablespoon of kim chee base and blend until the mixture is smooth and creamy. If you would like a more intense flavor, add more kim chee base, but be careful not to add too much, or your spread will become runny.

3. Serve as a dip or spread, or use as a topping for anything that could use a little kick.

BLACK BEAN PORTOBELLO MUSHROOMS WITH BABY BOK CHOY

4 large portobello
mushrooms, stemmed

2 tablespoons olive oil

4 baby bok choy, rinsed
and patted dry

4 teaspoons black bean sauce

1 tablespoon toasted
sesame seeds (optional)

❀

Prep time: 15 minutes
Grill time: 4 minutes
Serves: 4

My grandma Dora worked wonders with black bean sauce. She used it on tomato beef, chicken and green beans, and tofu and vegetables. While she made her own sauce, I often use store-bought, but either works great in this dish with baby bok choy.

1. Preheat a clean and oiled grill to medium heat.

2. Brush both sides of the mushrooms and all parts of the bok choy with olive oil.

3. Brush each mushroom top with 1 teaspoon of black bean sauce. Place the mushrooms on the grill, tops up.

4. Place the bok choy on the grill.

5. Turn the mushrooms and bok choy after about 2 minutes, and grill for another 2 minutes.

6. Remove the vegetables from the heat. Serve the mushrooms over the grilled bok choy. Sprinkle with sesame seeds, if using.

BEEF

PŪLEHU TRI-TIP

4 (8-ounce) tri-tip steaks

⅓ cup 'alaea (red Hawaiian) salt or kosher salt

1 tablespoon sugar

2 teaspoons fresh ground pepper

2 tablespoons minced fresh garlic

½ cup shoyu

2 teaspoons minced fresh ginger (optional)

1 tablespoon sesame oil (optional)

❀

Prep time: 15 minutes
Grill time: 6 to 10 minutes
Serves: 4 as a main

Pūlehu is the Hawaiian word meaning "to broil over a fire." To use this method, simply rub the steak with seasonings and then place it on the grill. This recipe is adapted from *Hawai'i Magazine*.

1. Preheat a clean and oiled grill to medium heat.

2. In a medium bowl, mix all the ingredients except for the steak.

3. Rub the mixture onto the steak.

4. Grill the steak for 3 to 5 minutes on each side.

KALBI SHORT RIBS

½ cup brown sugar

2 tablespoons minced
fresh garlic

1½ teaspoons minced
fresh ginger

2 tablespoons rice wine (mirin)

1 tablespoon sesame oil

½ cup shoyu

¼ cup water

1½ to 2 pounds kalbi short ribs

¼ cup diced green
onions, to garnish

❀

Prep time: 15 minutes
Marinate: Overnight
Grill time: 6 to 8 minutes
Serves: 2 as a main, 4 as a side

Korean barbecue delivers the ultra-satisfying flavor combination of sweet and salty. Most Asian markets carry ribs cut kalbi style, but if you don't see them at your local store, ask the butcher to cut them "flanken" style. This cut is thin and allows for quick grilling. Pairs perfectly with Classic Mac Salad (page 86) and steamed rice.

1. To make the marinade, mix all of the ingredients except for the short ribs and the green onions in a medium bowl.

2. Place the beef in a plastic zip-top bag and pour the marinade over it.

3. Marinate in the refrigerator overnight but no longer.

4. Preheat a clean and oiled grill to medium heat.

5. Remove the ribs from the marinade.

6. Grill for 3 to 4 minutes on each side.

7. Garnish with diced green onions.

GRILLED FLANK STEAK

1 bunch green onions,
thinly sliced, divided

1 tablespoon sugar

1 tablespoon sesame oil

2 tablespoons rice vinegar

½ cup shoyu

3 cloves garlic, minced

2 tablespoons peeled,
grated fresh ginger

½ teaspoon cayenne pepper

1 (1½- to 2-pound)
beef flank steak

2 tablespoons hot water

❀

Prep time: 15 minutes
Marinate: 2 hours to overnight
Grill time: 12 to 16 minutes
Serves: 4

You don't have to ask "Where's the beef?" anymore. This steak marinates in as little as 2 hours, making a tasty dinner that requires minimal planning. This steak pairs excellently with the Crispy Carrots with Hawaiian Sea Salt (page 43) and Grilled Romaine Salad with Fresh Mango (page 96).

1. Set aside ¼ cup of the sliced onions for garnish.

2. In a small bowl, whisk together the sugar, sesame oil, rice vinegar, shoyu, garlic, ginger, and cayenne pepper to make the marinade.

3. Set aside 2 to 3 tablespoons of the marinade for later. Transfer the remaining marinade into a resealable plastic bag.

4. Place the remaining green onions and steak into the resealable bag, turning the bag to coat them as you press out excess air and seal the bag.

5. Place the bag in the refrigerator for 2 hours to overnight, turning it over numerous times.

6. Preheat a clean and oiled grill to medium heat.

7. Remove the steak from the marinade. Grill the steak, covered, for 6 to 8 minutes, turning it over midway.

8. Remove the steak when it reaches your desired level of doneness, then let it rest 10 minutes.

9. Add 2 tablespoons of hot water to the reserved marinade. Drizzle it over the steak and sprinkle the reserved green onions on top of the steak.

GRILLED RIB EYE STEAK

Grilled rib eye is versatile: you can serve it as an entrée, offer pieces as pupus, or slice it over a mixed green salad.

1. To make the marinade, whisk together the pineapple juice, shoyu, apple cider vinegar, brown sugar, garlic, and ginger.

2. Place the steaks in 1- or 2-gallon-size zip-top bags. Pour the marinade over the meat and coat it evenly. Squeeze out excess air from the bag(s) prior to sealing.

3. Refrigerate for 40 minutes to overnight.

4. Preheat a clean and oiled grill to medium-high heat.

5. Remove the steaks from the marinade and discard the marinade.

6. Grill the steaks for 4 to 6 minutes per side for a 1- to 1½-inch steak.

7. Remove the steaks from the heat, top with parsley, if using, and enjoy.

⅔ cup pineapple juice

2 tablespoons low-sodium shoyu

2 tablespoons apple cider vinegar

1 tablespoon packed brown sugar

2 large cloves garlic, finely chopped

2 teaspoons grated fresh ginger

4 (10- to 12-ounce) boneless rib eye steaks

1 tablespoon chopped parsley (optional), to garnish

❀

Prep time: **15 minutes**
Marinate: **40 minutes**
Grill time: **8 to 12 minutes** each side
Serves: **4**

TERI BEEF STICKS

⅓ cup shoyu

3 tablespoons brown sugar

2 tablespoons white sugar

2 tablespoons water

1 teaspoon minced fresh garlic

½ teaspoon minced fresh ginger

1 pound flank or skirt steak, sliced into 2 x ¼-inch strips; if you want to skip cutting the meat, use stir-fry beef instead

skewers (soak wooden skewers in warm water for 30 minutes prior to use)

❀

Prep time: 15 minutes
Marinate: Overnight
Grill time: 6 to 10 minutes
Serves: 2 as a main, 4 as a side

These are the flavors that got me hooked on eating anything off a skewer as a kid and then brought me back to beef after living as a vegetarian for the first two years of college. You can cook these tasty skewers on a full-size grill, or, as we do at the beach here often, on a portable charcoal barbecue grill called a hibachi. This recipe is courtesy of Tess Bevernage, my sister-in-law, and Thomas Robillard, my brother, of the Vancouver-based catering company Hānai Family Table.

1. Mix all of the ingredients except for steak in a medium bowl to make the marinade.

2. Place the beef in a large glass bowl with a cover or a plastic zip-top bag. Pour the marinade over the beef.

3. Cover and marinate the beef in the refrigerator overnight but no longer. If you are using wooden skewers, soak them in water overnight so they don't catch fire on the grill.

4. Preheat a clean and oiled grill to medium heat.

5. Thread the meat onto the skewers by gently pushing the skewer through each end of each piece.

6. Grill on medium heat for about 3 minutes or longer on each side, depending on the thickness of the meat. Serve with mac salad or over a green salad.

PICNIC AND PARTY

GRILLED CHEESE ON SWEET BREAD

2 tablespoons butter

8 slices sweet bread, evenly sliced

1 (12-ounce) package sliced cheese

❀

Prep time: **10 minutes**
Grill time: **4 to 6 minutes**
Serves: **4**

For fans who appreciate the salty and sweet, this take on the classic grilled cheese sandwich delivers. Punalu'u Bake Shop on the Big Island bakes long loaves that are perfect for slicing thick and making grilled cheese sandwiches. You can also use homemade bread or another store-bought bread.

1. Preheat a clean and oiled grill to medium heat.

2. Butter each slice of bread.

3. Place the buttered bread onto the heated grill. Place 1 to 2 slices of cheese and the second slice of bread on top.

4. Close the grill lid for about 2 to 3 minutes.

5. Flip the sandwiches over and grill until cheese has melted.

6. Remove from the heat and enjoy.

TACO BAR

Almost as a rule, my auntie Shirley orders appetizers as her main meal—a little bit of this and a little bit of that—when we dine at restaurants. Enjoying favorite tastes is the theme of this taco bar, where the servings are small so you can try different flavors, all of them delicious. For small kine 'ono grinds, or appetizers, make taco fillings by grilling some Pūlehu Tri-Tip (page 49), Lemongrass Swordfish (page 36), or Teri Chicken Skewers (page 14), place them on top of your favorite tortillas, and top with Charred Salsa or homemade Guacamole.

CHARRED SALSA

1 small ripe mango or 1 pound frozen mango pieces, thawed

8 to 10 cherry tomatoes (about ½ cup)

1 to 2 red or yellow bell peppers, halved, seeds removed

½ medium red onion, sliced into rounds

¼ cup chopped Chinese parsley leaves

1 tablespoon red wine vinegar

Hawaiian salt, to taste

skewers (soak wooden skewers in warm water for 30 minutes prior to use)

❀

Prep time: 10 minutes
Grill time: 5 to 7 minutes
Serves: 4 to 6

1. Preheat a clean and oiled grill to medium heat.

2. If you are using fresh mango (highly recommended, as the taste and texture are better), peel the mango and cut it into thick slices. If you are using frozen mango chunks, thread them onto skewers or spread them in an even layer in a grill basket.

3. Thread the cherry tomatoes onto skewers.

4. Place the bell peppers, tomatoes, red onion, and mango on the grill. Flipping to cook both sides evenly, grill the vegetables and fruit until they are charred on both sides.

5. Remove the vegetables from the grill, and rub off any easily removed skin from the bell peppers.

6. Finely dice all of the grilled vegetables, and combine them in a medium bowl with the Chinese parsley, red wine vinegar, and Hawaiian salt.

7. Adjust the seasoning to your preference and serve warm. You can also make this in advance and serve it chilled.

GUACAMOLE

2 cups mashed avocado

1 red onion, peeled and diced

juice of 1 lime

2 cloves garlic, minced

2 tablespoons chopped
Chinese parsley leaves

½ teaspoon Hawaiian
or kosher salt

Prep time: 10 minutes
Serves: 4

In Hawai'i the avocados often grow to the size of cantaloupes.
This is what I like to do with them.

1. Combine the avocado, red onion, lime juice, garlic, parsley,
   and salt in a medium bowl.

2. Serve over tacos and as a dip for your chips.

HAMAJANG HOT DOGS

You never know who might come by, so it's best to be ready to offer something to eat. Only have hot dogs on hand? Then you're all set. In local slang, *hamajang* means "all mixed up," and you can mix and match this variety of hot dog choices and toppings any way you like. We started with local favorites—shoyu-style hot dogs, Redondo's red hot dogs, and Portuguese sausage—and added Bacon and Onion Topping, Sriracha Aioli, kim chee, and Charred Salsa.

1. Preheat a clean and oiled grill to medium heat.

2. Place the hot dogs on the heated grill, and turn them after 3 to 4 minutes.

3. Place the grilled hot dogs in buns and top with desired toppings.

assorted hot dogs, such as Redondo's red hot dogs, Portuguese sausages, or your personal favorite

hot dog buns

Bacon and Onion Topping (page 65), Sriracha Aioli (page 65), Charred Salsa (page 60), and other assorted toppings

❀

Prep time: **15 minutes**
Grill time: **6 to 8 minutes, longer for jumbo dogs**
Serves: **4**

SHOYU DOGS

Shoyu hot dogs are a local classic—a little salty, a little sweet—good on their own or stuffed in a bun.

1. Preheat a clean and oiled grill to medium heat.

2. Combine the shoyu and brown sugar in a small bowl until the sugar fully dissolves.

3. Place the hot dogs on the grill, brushing them with the shoyu and sugar marinade.

4. Turn the dogs after 2 to 3 minutes, then continue to grill until done, about 2 to 3 minutes more.

½ cup shoyu

3 tablespoons packed brown sugar

1 (8- to 12-count) package hot dogs

hot dog buns

❀

Prep time: **5 minutes**
Grill time: **5 to 6 minutes**
Serves: **8 to 12**

BACON AND ONION TOPPING

This favorite topping of my Grandma Dora Gin goes great on hot dogs fresh off the grill, or add the hot dogs right into the frying pan with the topping and eat.

½ (12-ounce) package uncooked bacon

½ onion, diced

¼ cup ketchup

1 teaspoon shoyu

Prep time: **15 minutes**
Serves: **4**

1. Fry the bacon on the stovetop. Once crispy, remove the bacon from the pan and place it on a plate lined with paper towels to drain. Slice the bacon into ½-inch pieces.

2. Fry the onions in the pan with the bacon grease.

3. Add the ketchup, shoyu, and bacon pieces to the onions.

SRIRACHA AIOLI

This spicy mayo tastes great on hot dogs, hamburgers, and veggies. Add a healthy pile of kim chee to give your dog even more of a spicy kick. (It's a great substitute for sauerkraut and pairs exceptionally well with the Portuguese sausages.)

4 tablespoons mayonnaise

2 teaspoons sriracha

Prep time: **5 minutes**
Serves: **8**

In a small bowl, combine the mayonnaise and sriracha. Add more sriracha for more spice.

GRILLED SPAM MUSUBI

Here we eat Spam Musubi after soccer tournaments, at baseball games, in the middle of hiking Maunawili Falls, at class parties, at school events, and when we just need something 'ono to fill our bellies. It's available in single servings for purchase at 7-Eleven, at most grocery stores, and at every school event and fundraiser. Chances are, my son has one in his backpack right now. This is a grilled twist on the traditional shoyu-sugar variety. For a vegetarian option, you can substitute the Spam with 1 (15-ounce) container of firm tofu, sliced into 8 pieces.

3 cups short-grain rice like Calrose

3 cups water

¼ cup shoyu

½ cup sugar

1 (12-ounce) can Spam, sliced lengthwise into 8 pieces

5 sheets of nori seaweed, trimmed to wrap around each piece

furikake (optional)

※

Prep time: **30 minutes**
Marinate: **10 to 15 minutes**
Grill time: **6 to 10 minutes**
Serves: **8**

1. Preheat a clean and oiled grill to medium heat.

2. Cook the rice in a rice cooker or on the stove with the water. Allow the rice to cool to room temperature for handling.

3. Combine the shoyu and sugar in a medium bowl until the sugar dissolves to create the marinade.

4. Place the Spam slices in a pan and coat them evenly with the marinade. Marinate the Spam for 10 to 15 minutes.

5. Remove the Spam from the marinade and grill each side for about 3 to 5 minutes, until grill marks develop. Remove from the heat.

Tip: If you don't have a musubi mold, you can make your own. Clean out the Spam can and use a can opener to remove the bottom of the can.

6. If you're taking your Spam musubi to go and want to enclose it in plastic wrap, place the plastic wrap down first, then the nori. Lay strips of nori seaweed shiny side down on a flat, dry working surface.

7. Place a musubi press or Spam can in the center of the seaweed. Have a small bowl of water handy for keeping your fingers wet to avoid rice sticking to you.

8. Spoon about ⅔ cup of cooked rice into the press or can, and pack the rice down tightly until it's about 1 inch tall. Pull up the press or can, keeping the rice on the nori.

9. Place a grilled Spam slice on top of the block of rice. Fold one end of the seaweed between the Spam and rice, and then moisten the underside of the other end of the seaweed and seal the seaweed together. Sprinkle with furikake, if using.

TERI BURGERS

If Hānai Family Table's teri burgers are on the grill, there's going to be a scoop of 'ono mac salad on your plate. Top your burger with sliced tomato and cheddar cheese, or just savor the meat in the bun. Recipe courtesy of Tess Bevernage and Thomas Robillard.

1. Mix the first six ingredients together in a medium bowl to make the marinade. Set aside 2 teaspoons of the marinade to add to the mayo plus 2 tablespoons for basting on the grill.

2. Place the ground beef in a zip-top bag and pour the marinade over it. Marinate in the refrigerator overnight but no longer, to avoid the meat getting mushy.

3. Preheat a clean and oiled grill to medium heat.

4. Form beef into balls slightly smaller than a tennis ball. One pound of beef makes 4 burgers.

5. Flatten the raw beef with your palm so that it is slightly larger than the hamburger bun. The teri burger will be thin and shrink when grilled.

6. Grill the patties for about 3 minutes on each side, basting them with the 2 tablespoons of reserved marinade. Toast the hamburger buns (optional).

7. Spread the mayo mixed with 2 teaspoons of marinade onto the hamburger buns and make your teri burgers.

¼ cup white sugar

¼ cup brown sugar

½ cup shoyu

1 teaspoon minced fresh garlic

1 teaspoon minced fresh ginger (use your Parmesan grater or other cheese grater)

¼ cup water

1 pound ground beef

hamburger buns

⅓ cup mayonnaise

❀

Prep time: 15 minutes
Marinate: Overnight but no longer
Grill time: 6 to 7 minutes
Serves: 4

PORK

GINGER AND GARLIC PORK CHOPS

¾ cup shoyu

⅓ cup brown sugar

3 tablespoons fresh lemon juice (1 large lemon)

2 tablespoons vegetable oil

1 teaspoon ground ginger

¼ teaspoon garlic powder

6 pork chops, bone in or bone out

❀

Prep time: **15 minutes**
Marinate: **6 hours to overnight**
Grill time: **12 to 16 minutes**
Serves: **6**

These pork chops go well with coleslaw or applesauce. The marinade doesn't require any chopping because it uses garlic and ginger powder. I've adapted this recipe from Ben's Chinese Pork Chops on Allrecipes.com.

1. To make the marinade, mix all of the ingredients except for the pork in a large bowl. Reserve ¼ cup of the marinade for basting.

2. Pierce the pork chops two or three times on both sides with a fork.

3. Place the pork chops in a gallon-size zip-top bag and pour the marinade over them, coating the pork chops evenly. Refrigerate for 6 hours to overnight.

4. Preheat a clean and oiled grill to high heat.

5. Remove the pork chops from the marinade and grill for 6 to 8 minutes per side, basting often with the ¼ cup of reserved marinade.

ADOBO PORK BELLY BAO
WITH WON BOK SLAW

⅔ cup light shoyu

⅓ cup white vinegar

3 bay leaves

1 tablespoon whole
black peppercorns

3 cloves garlic, roughly chopped

2 tablespoons white sugar

1 (1-pound) piece thin-cut,
skinless pork belly, cut into
2-inch strips, excess fat trimmed

1 bunch green onions, cut
lengthwise into
2- to 3-inch-long pieces

4 to 6 bao buns

skewers (soak wooden
skewers in warm water for
30 minutes prior to use)

❀

Prep time: 20 minutes
Marinate: 2 hours to overnight
Grill time: 15 minutes
Serves: 3 to 4

Asian grocery stores often stock fresh or frozen folded bao buns, perfect for stuffing with this delicious pork belly filling and coleslaw. If you don't have access to the ready-made buns, there are recipes online for making them at home. Vegetarians can substitute tofu in place of the pork belly.

1. To make the marinade, combine the shoyu, white vinegar, bay leaves, whole black peppercorns, garlic, and sugar in a medium bowl.

2. Place the pork belly in a zip-top bag or other container with a lid, cover with the marinade, and refrigerate for at least 2 hours but preferably overnight. If the meat is not completely covered, flip it at least once while marinating.

3. Preheat a clean and oiled grill to medium heat.

4. Remove the belly from the marinade and brush off any loose bits, such as peppercorns or the bay leaves from the marinade. Weave the pork belly onto metal skewers. Place the skewers on the grate, and cook the pork for about 10 minutes on each side.

5. Place the pork belly into warm bao buns. Top with Won Bok Slaw.

WON BOK SLAW

1. Place the green onions in a small bowl of ice water to create curling.

2. In a large bowl, combine the sugar, fish sauce, sesame oil, shoyu, and Chinese parsley.

3. Toss in the won bok.

4. Add green onions.

¼ cup green onions, chopped into
2- to 3-inch strips and then cut thin

1 tablespoon sugar

1 teaspoon fish sauce

1 teaspoon sesame oil

2 tablespoons shoyu

2 tablespoons Chinese parsley
leaves, chopped

2 cups thinly chopped won bok
(Chinese cabbage)

ISLAND-STYLE CHAR SIU
BABY BACK RIBS

As Mark Bittman remarks in *How to Grill Everything*, Char Siu Baby Back Ribs are great for anyone new to grilling ribs. The char siu flavor is reminiscent of the char siu bao, or pork buns, the manapua (the Hawaiian name for char siu bao) man used to sell here in Hawai'i out of an ice cream truck–like white van. After school we'd hand a quarter through the fence at school and the manapua man would give us a rice cake or manapua.

1. Preheat a clean and oiled grill to medium-low heat.

2. Season the ribs with salt and pepper on both sides.

3. To make the sauce, combine the hoisin sauce, honey, shoyu, rice wine, ginger, and five-spice powder in a small bowl and whisk together. Set aside.

4. Place the ribs, meaty side up, on the grill and close the lid. Maintain a temperature between 250° and 300°F and cook for about an hour, then brush sauce on both sides of the ribs.

5. Continue grilling the ribs, turning and moving the rack every 30 minutes and adding glaze each time.

6. Grill until it's easy to cut between two ribs with a sharp knife, 1½ to 2½ hours total.

1 (4-pound) rack baby back ribs

salt and pepper, to taste

¼ cup hoisin sauce

¼ cup honey

¼ cup shoyu

2 tablespoons rice wine

1 tablespoon minced
fresh ginger

¼ teaspoon five-spice powder

❀

Prep time: **15 minutes**
Grill time: **1½ to 2½ hours**
Serves: **4 to 6**

SHISO PORK SKEWERS

Many yakitori places serve grilled pork with shiso, and it's one of Dawn's family favorites. This is her recipe for a homemade version. Shiso is fairly easy to find at Japanese or Asian markets. Look for thin-cut pork that has a nice amount of fat (not too lean—it ends up too dry), but not as much fat as belly cuts. Our local market sells a cut labeled "thin-cut pork steak," a great mix of meat and fat. Whatever you get, it needs to be boneless and about ⅛ inch thick.

1. Preheat a clean and oiled grill to high heat. Presoak your skewers, if using wooden ones.

2. Lay 2 or 3 pieces of pork next to each other, creating a large "pork rectangle" roughly the size of a sheet of printer paper. If the edges of your pieces aren't completely straight, layer them slightly so that you have no gaps where they touch. Season lightly with garlic salt and pepper.

3. Lay the shiso leaves over the pork, spacing them fairly close together. (Shiso has an intense taste, so you may prefer to space them more widely, using fewer leaves; my family loves it, so we pack them in closely, with almost no gaps.)

4. Carefully roll the pork and shiso up like a jelly roll. Roll tightly to prevent it from falling apart during the skewering and grilling process. You should end up with a log about 2 inches in diameter and 10 to 12 inches long. Repeat Steps 2 to 4 until all pork is used up.

5. Slice rolls into pieces about ½ inch thick. Skewer the rounds through their diameter; about 5 or 6 should fit per skewer. Season each side of the skewered pieces with Hawaiian salt.

6. Grill over high heat, about 4 to 6 minutes per side, until lightly charred. The pork skewers will cook fast and if your pork is particularly fatty, they will flare up! Serve immediately.

1½ to 2 pounds boneless, thin-cut pork (about ⅛ inch thick)

garlic salt and pepper, to taste

12 to 20 shiso leaves

Hawaiian salt, to taste

skewers (soak wooden skewers in warm water for 30 minutes prior to use)

❀

Prep time: 20 minutes
Grill time: 8 to 12 minutes
Serves: 4 to 6

Note: A tonkatsu cut with a good amount of fat in the pork works well. Cuts meant for sukiyaki are too thin and not fatty enough. Otherwise, a meat mallet is your best friend; find the thinnest cut of pork you can and pound out your stress.

DESSERTS

DA KINE S'MORES

1 bag jumbo marshmallows

2 to 3 giant Hershey's
Milk Chocolate bars

Diamond Bakery Royal Creem
Crackers (or graham crackers)

skewers (soak wooden
skewers in warm water for
30 minutes prior to use)

❀

Prep time: **10 minutes**
Grill time: **2 to 4 minutes**
Serves: **4 to 10**

Diamond Bakery in Hawai'i makes a crisp alternative to traditional graham crackers called Royal Creem Crackers. They come in a variety of flavors, including coconut and Kona coffee, as well as classic. MarieLu biscuits (cookies) work if you can't find Diamond Bakery goods and don't have time to order online. S'mores come out best when cooked over an open flame, so bring on the charcoal. We use a small Smokey Joe.

1. Preheat a clean and oiled charcoal grill.

2. Place a marshmallow on the end of a long skewer.

3. Hold the marshmallow close to the open flame, turning it as it browns.

4. When the marshmallow is good and roasted, 2 to 4 minutes, place it with a piece of chocolate between two crackers.

GRILLED BANANA WITH TOASTED COCONUT

2 bananas, halved lengthwise

2 tablespoons olive oil

4 tablespoons toasted, shredded coconut

1 tablespoon cocoa nibs (optional)

2 tablespoons crushed macadamia nuts (optional)

1 can whipped cream or 1 cup fresh whipped cream

❀

Prep time: 10 minutes
Grill time: 4 to 6 minutes total
Serves: 4

In Hawai'i, our local bananas are called apple bananas. They are smaller and more tart than the typical bananas available on the mainland. We have bananas growing in our side yard, sometimes in bunches of more than 70. We cut off hands and give them to friends and neighbors, family, and soccer teammates. This recipe works with any kind of firm banana (very ripe, mushy bananas will melt into the grill).

1. Preheat a clean and oiled grill to medium heat.

2. Brush the bananas with olive oil on both sides.

3. Place the bananas on the grill and cook for 2 to 3 minutes on each side.

4. Remove the bananas from the heat.

5. Place each half-banana slice onto a plate, and sprinkle with coconut, cocoa nibs, if using, and mac nuts, if desired. Top with whipped cream.

SPICY LI HING MUI PINEAPPLE

½ teaspoon li hing mui powder

¼ teaspoon chili powder (optional)

¼ teaspoon cayenne pepper (optional)

2 tablespoons olive oil

1 pineapple, peeled and cut into spears

1 tablespoon fresh mint leaves, to garnish (optional)

4 cups vanilla ice cream

❀

Prep time: 30 minutes
Grill time: 4 to 6 minutes
Serves: 4 to 8

Warm, grilled pineapple is to die for. Add popular li hing mui powder, made from dried, salted plums, which is readily available in the snack aisles here in the Islands and online worldwide. Sprinkle a mix of cayenne pepper and chili powder for a spicy kick and surprise to the taste buds. Serve over vanilla ice cream to perfectly pair sweet with sour.

1. Preheat a clean and oiled grill to medium heat.

2. Mix the li hing mui powder, chili powder, and cayenne pepper, if using.

3. Lightly brush the olive oil onto the pineapple spears.

4. Place the pineapple spears onto the heated grill. Turn after 2 to 3 minutes and grill for just as long on the other side, making sure not to dry out the pineapple.

5. Remove the pineapple from the heat and transfer to a plate. Sprinkle with the li hing and pepper mixture.

6. To serve, sprinkle with mint leaves, if using, and 1 scoop of vanilla ice cream.

GRILLED SWEET BREAD WITH MANGO

8 slices sweet bread,
sliced evenly

2 tablespoons butter

2 fresh mangoes,
sliced into planks

2 tablespoons olive oil

fresh or canned whipped
cream, to serve

fresh mint leaves
(optional), to serve

❀

Prep time: 10 minutes
Grill time: 3 to 4 minutes
Serves: 4

Did you know that Hawaiian sweet bread is actually an import from Portuguese immigrants who came to the Islands in the 1800s to work the ranches and plantations? We used the guava-flavored Hawaiian sweet bread from Punalu'u Bake Shop but you can use any sweet bread cut into 1-inch slices.

1. Preheat a clean and oiled grill to medium heat.

2. Butter both sides of each bread slice.

3. Brush each mango plank with olive oil.

4. Place the buttered bread and the mango slices onto the heated grill.

5. Close the grill lid and cook for 1½ to 2 minutes.

6. Flip over the bread and mango, and grill for 1 to 2 minutes more, being careful not to burn them.

7. Remove the bread and mango from the heat.

8. Top each slice of bread with 1 slice of grilled mango, whipped cream, and mint leaves, if using, to serve.

SIDES

FURIKAKE PARTY MIX

¼ cup butter

¼ cup light corn syrup

¼ cup vegetable oil

¼ cup sugar

1 tablespoon shoyu

1 (12.3-ounce) package bite-size corn and wheat cereal squares

furikake nori

❀

Prep time: **15 minutes**
Cook time: **45 minutes**
Makes: **12 (1-cup) servings**

This is an Island take on the popular Chex Party Mix. This recipe is based on a variation found in *A Hundred Years of Island Cooking: a Collection of Recipes from Hawaiian Electric Company.*

1. Preheat the oven to 250°F.

2. In a small saucepan, melt the butter.

3. Add the corn syrup, vegetable oil, sugar, and shoyu, and stir until the sugar dissolves.

4. Spread the cereal out on a large, foil-lined baking pan.

5. Pour the syrup over the cereal, coating it evenly.

6. Stir in the furikake nori.

7. Bake for 15 minutes, then stir. Do this two more times for a total baking time of 45 minutes.

8. Cool and store in an airtight container.

CLASSIC MAC SALAD

8 ounces elbow macaroni

2 hard-boiled eggs

1 tablespoon white vinegar

½ medium carrot, grated on the large side of a box grater (about ½ cup)

1 to 2 tablespoons finely grated Maui or 'Ewa or any variety of sweet onion

1 to 2 cups mayonnaise

salt, pepper, and no-salt herb seasoning (such as Mrs. Dash), to taste

paprika

❀

Prep time: 6 minutes
Cook time: 7 to 8 minutes
Serves: 4 to 6

Local-style mac salad usually runs to a mayonnaise extreme, and brands tend to differ wildly when it comes to consistency and flavor; if you're not a big fan of the condiment, start with 1 cup and see how you feel about the texture and taste.

Macaroni salad is a Hawai'i lunch plate essential, and you'll find it at most potluck parties. The creamy mayonnaise is the perfect complement to salty, smoky grilled meats. The salad can be made with endless variations. Start with this basic, classic version adapted from *Kau Kau: Cuisine and Culture in the Hawaiian Islands*, and feel free to add your own twist; change up the pasta type, add peas, potatoes, tuna—anything you think sounds good. All ingredient amounts are intended to be adjusted to your taste—if you think something sounds like too much, start with less and add more until you're happy.

1. Cook the elbow macaroni according to package directions and drain; traditionally, mac salad is soft, but you can go with a more al dente cook, if you like.

2. Separate the egg yolks from the whites. Mash the egg yolks and set aside. Dice the egg whites and add them with the drained macaroni to a large bowl.

3. Add the vinegar, carrot, and onion. Mix gently to incorporate the ingredients.

4. Add the mayo and mix thoroughly.

5. Season to taste with salt, pepper, and herb seasoning. Chill overnight to allow the flavors to meld thoroughly.

6. Add a dusting of paprika before serving.

FAST AND EASY FRIED NOODLES

This potluck hit comes from Janet Sakamoto, our photographer's mom. Fried noodles are a local staple and a perfect accompaniment for all sorts of grilled foods. You can use any assortment of vegetables that you like, and in any amount—the ingredient list below is a jumping-off point; adjust to your preference. S&S brand saimin noodles are *highly* recommended; the frozen 'Ohana 9-Pack (see Resources section) is enough to make two batches. Wok oil adds a terrific garlic-ginger taste.

1. Thaw the noodles by running them briefly under hot water and gently shaking them until they separate. Drain them thoroughly. Noodles should be loose, but not soft and mushy, as the heat of the pan will soften them.

2. Heat a large wok (or other deep pan suitable for stir-frying) over medium-high heat. If you are using Spam, you don't need to add any oil; if you are not, add a tablespoon of oil.

3. When the wok is hot, add the Spam, if using, and fry it until it begins to turn a light golden-brown.

4. Add your vegetables and the contents of one soup base packet. Stir-fry until the onion begins to turn translucent.

5. Add the drained saimin noodles. Season with 1 or 2 additional soup base packets; these are very salty, so add seasoning according to your taste.

6. Add a dash of shoyu—some people like their noodles very salty and on the darker brown end of the spectrum; we prefer a lighter hand with the shoyu.

7. Mix the noodles and vegetables together gently, so as not to break the noodles. The easiest way to do this is by employing a "pick-up-and-drop" technique using a pair of tongs.

8. Add the kamaboko and green onions and mix lightly again.

9. Transfer to a serving dish and garnish with Chinese parsley.

4 (4.5-ounce) packages frozen saimin noodles with soup base seasoning packets

wok oil (or peanut or canola oil), for frying (if you are omitting Spam)

½ (12-ounce) can Spam, cut into ¼-inch-thick matchsticks (optional)

2 stalks celery, julienned 1⁄16 to ⅛ inch thick, 2 inches long on the bias

¼ medium Maui or 'Ewa or any variety of sweet onion, julienned 1⁄16 to ⅛ inch thick, 2 inches long

½ medium carrot, julienned 1⁄16 to ⅛ inch thick, 2 inches long

dash of shoyu

½ (5.5- or 6-ounce) block kamaboko, cut into ¼-inch-thick matchsticks

4 to 5 stalks green onion, minced

Chinese parsley, leaves and minced stems, to garnish

❀

Prep time: 20 minutes
Cook time: 10 minutes
Serves: 4 as a main dish or 8 to 10 as a side

DRINKS

GUAVA PUNCH

1 cup fresh guava puree plus ¾ cup sugar OR 1 can any variation of frozen guava concentrate OR 3 (11.5-ounce) cans any variation of guava drinks

3 cups water (if not using canned drinks or concentrate)

¾ cup orange juice

½ cup pineapple juice

¼ cup lemon juice (1 large lemon)

2 cups sparkling water

1 cup rum (optional)

pineapple wedges (optional)

❀

Prep time: **10 minutes**

Serves: **6**

My neighbor grows beautiful guavas, which we use for the Guava Chicken recipe (page 16) as well as making this punch with frozen guava puree from her tree. But you don't have to have access to fresh guavas to make this refreshing drink. The recipe is adapted from Fresh Guava Fruit Punch in *Fruits of Hawaii*, by Carey D. Miller, Katherine Bazore, and Mary Bartow.

1. Thaw the frozen guava concentrate, if using.

2. Pour the guava into a pitcher with all of the remaining ingredients except for the pineapple wedges, and stir.

3. Garnish each glass with a pineapple wedge, if using, and serve over ice.

PLANTATION ICED TEA

6½ cups unsweetened tea

grilled lemon slices (optional)

4 cups unsweetened
pineapple juice

fresh mint leaves (optional)

orchid (optional)

❀

Prep time: 10 minutes
Cook time: 3 minutes
Serves: 6

Whether you brew your own tea or buy ready-made, this blend
of subtle and sweet and the dramatic contrast of color in your
cup will wow. Grilling the lemon brings out a sweetness and
adds a surprising smoky dimension.

1. Brew the tea if it's not ready-made. Allow it to cool.

2. Grill lemon slices for about a minute on each side, or until
you see grill marks.

3. Combine the tea and pineapple juice. Add the grilled
lemon slices.

4. Garnish with mint leaves and a decorative orchid, if using.

SALADS

GRILLED BREAD SALAD

¾ cup olive oil, divided

2 tablespoons balsamic vinegar

ciabatta or French loaf, cut
into 1-inch-thick slices

1 container cherry tomatoes

Hawaiian 'alaea sea salt
or kosher salt, to taste

1 Portuguese or other
sausage (optional)

4 cups mixed greens

½ red onion, sliced
into 1-inch pieces

skewers (soak wooden
skewers in warm water for
30 minutes prior to use)

❀

Prep time: 10 minutes
Grill time: 20 minutes
Serves: 4

The plantation culture that heavily influenced the cuisine of the Islands taught people to use whatever ingredients were on hand, including leftovers, to make meals. Stale bread works just fine for this recipe. Once it's toasted it gives this salad a crunch.

1. Preheat a clean and oiled grill to high heat.

2. In a small bowl, whisk together ¼ cup of olive oil and balsamic vinegar. Set aside.

3. Brush some of the remaining olive oil on both sides of the bread slices.

4. Slide the cherry tomatoes onto skewers. Brush them with the remaining olive oil and sprinkle them with salt.

5. Place the sausage on the grill for 1 to 2 minutes to brown it. Turn down the heat to medium, and grill for about 10 to 15 minutes more.

6. Once the sausage has been on the grill for about 10 minutes and turned, place the cherry tomatoes and slices of bread onto the grill. Turn the bread after about 30 seconds and the tomatoes after 2 to 3 minutes.

7. Remove the tomatoes, bread, and sausage from the heat.

8. Cut the bread into cubes.

9. Toss the mixed greens and red onion with the olive oil and balsamic dressing. Fold in the sausage, bread cubes, and grilled tomatoes.

GRILLED ROMAINE SALAD WITH FRESH MANGO

4 heads romaine lettuce, top and base trimmed off ¼ to ½ inch

⅓ cup olive oil

2 tablespoons Hawaiian 'alaea, sea, or kosher salt

2 fresh mangoes, thinly sliced

1 tablespoon balsamic vinegar

❀

Prep time: **5 minutes**
Grill time: **6 minutes**
Serves: **4**

Warm salad works like comfort food. It sounds weird to wilt your lettuce, but when you add oil and salt, it works. I promise.

1. Preheat a clean and oiled grill to low-medium heat.

2. Brush the lettuce on all sides with the olive oil. Sprinkle with ½ tablespoon of salt.

3. Place the lettuce on the grill. Cook for 3 minutes per side.

4. Remove the lettuce from the heat. Top it with fresh mango and sprinkle with the remaining salt, to taste, and balsamic vinegar.

SMASHED CUCUMBER SALAD

3 cloves garlic, diced

1 tablespoon rice vinegar

2 teaspoons low-sodium shoyu

½ teaspoon sugar

½ tablespoon sesame oil

½ teaspoon to ½ tablespoon
chili oil, to taste

thinly sliced Hawaiian
or Thai chili pepper

black sesame seeds (optional)

1 fresh English cucumber,
skin peeled halfway, ends
chopped, sliced into 3- to
4-inch pieces, and deseeded

salt, to taste

❀

Prep time: 5 minutes
Serves: 2 to 4

This salad comes together in just 5 minutes and adds a refreshing side to your hot grilled foods. Make it as spicy as you like. This recipe is adapted from Elaine's Chinese Cucumber Salad, found on her website ChinaSichuanFood.com.

1. To make the dressing, combine all of the ingredients except the cucumber, chili peppers, and sesame seeds evenly in a medium bowl.

2. Place the cucumber pieces on paper towels to absorb their water and to avoid having them slide away.

3. Smash each piece using the heel of your palm against the flat side of a wide kitchen knife or butcher knife until the cucumber pieces are well crushed.

4. Dice the smashed cucumber into single-bite pieces.

5. Mix the cucumber pieces with the dressing. Top with slivers of fresh peppers, black or tan sesame seeds, and salt, to taste.

'ULU AND 'UALA SALAD

1 cup peeled and cubed 'ulu, or breadfruit

1 pound Okinawan sweet potatoes or yellow sweet potatoes, peeled and cut into 1-inch chunks

2 tablespoons chopped Chinese parsley leaves

juice from 1 lime

1 tablespoon green onions, thinly sliced and chilled in ice water to curl (optional)

1 tablespoon grated ginger

salt and pepper, to taste

⅓ cup coconut cream

❀

Prep time: 15 minutes
Grill time: 6 minutes
Serves: 4

This recipe is based on one from CookingHawaiianStyle.com. If you do not have breadfruit, 'ulu, you can substitute jackfruit or taro. If you can't find either, make this sweet potato, or 'uala, salad anyway by simply doubling the sweet potatoes.

1. Preheat a clean and oiled grill to low-medium heat.

2. Place the breadfruit slices onto the grill and cook for 3 minutes per side. Remove the breadfruit from the heat.

3. In a large bowl, combine the sweet potatoes, 'ulu, parsley, lime juice, green onions, ginger, salt and pepper, and coconut cream. Toss until the 'ulu and sweet potatoes are coated.

4. Top with the green onions.

RESOURCES

All of the ingredients in these recipes are readily available here in Hawai'i at the stores listed below. We have also listed some mainland stores as a first stop for your shopping, but keep in mind that many ethnic stores, like Italian, Mexican, and Indian shops, may carry what you need as well. You can find every ingredient used in this book online.

Hawai'i

❀ Don Quijote
www.donquijotehawaii.com
This Japanese-based discount store is where you go to buy meat and veggies for the grill and end up buying an electric fly swatter and skincare products from Japan too. Open 24 hours a day, its competitive prices make a wide variety of Asian groceries readily available.

❀ Foodland
www.foodland.com
Hawai'i's largest locally owned and operated grocery retailer, Foodland is the store you remember from when you were 10 and would sneak li hing mui into the cart. With 34 locations across the Big Island, Maui, O'ahu, and Kaua'i, this store is a go-to for poke, mochi, local salsa, and all the national brands too.

❀ Marukai Wholesale Mart
www.marukaihawaii.com
Marukai's mission is to share Japanese traditions and the flavors of Japanese foods. You used to need a membership to shop—$15 for the first year and $10 thereafter—a bargain when you're buying fish cake, red beans, and a massage chair on your first visit, but now it's open to the public, no membership required.

❀ Safeway
www.safeway.com
The Hawai'i locations of this national chain reliably stock loaves of delicious Punalu'u bread, but they never seem to have apple bananas. You win some, you go to another store for what you can't find.

❀ Times Supermarket
www.timessupermarkets.com
With 17 locations across Maui, Oʻahu, and the Big Island, Times has been a favorite local market in Hawaiʻi since 1949. The smell from the Times market grill in the parking lot at the Kailua location draws in a good crowd to pick up lunch to go. They support local farms and local produce and Hawaiʻi-made products.

Mainland

❀ H Mart
www.hmart.com
With 97 locations across the US, this Korean full-service market delivers quality groceries and superior produce. Online ordering and delivery are available in certain areas.

❀ 99 Ranch Market
www.99ranch.com
If you're looking for Hawaiian Sun canned drinks, chances are your Ranch 99, or the one in the next town over, has them in stock. Asian pears too. Most locations also have a hot foods bar, where you can get your fill of steamed char siu bao and spicy eggplant.

❀ Uwajimaya (Pacific Northwest)
www.uwajimaya.com
Four locations in Washington and Oregon are stocked with products from Japan, China, Korea, Vietnam, Thailand, India, Indonesia, the Philippines, and beyond, making this a one-stop shop to satisfy all of your Asian cooking needs.

Online

❀ H Mart
www.hmart.com/shipping-delivery

❀ 99 Ranch Market
www.99ranch.com/shop

❀ Only from Hawaii
www.onlyfromhawaii.com
Offers a wide variety of beloved Hawaiʻi products and favorite local brands, including Halm's kim chee products, Hawaiian Sun juice, frozen S&S saimin noodles (you'll want the ʻOhana 9-pack to make our Fried Noodles on page 89!), Redondo's hot dogs, and Diamond Bakery crackers.

❀ Punaluʻu Bake Shop
www.bakeshophawaii.com

Books

Fruits of Hawaii by Carey D. Miller, Katherine Bazore, and Mary Bartow
Printed in 1965 by the University of Hawaiʻi Press, this book covers the fruits found in Hawaiʻi in historical perspective and discusses their edible qualities. Illustrations detail how to cut a pineapple, and the text clearly explains how to choose the best, so you're not guessing at the grocery store. The section on coconut includes recipes for chicken and shrimp curries, going beyond the book's primary focus on fruits. While currently out of print, copies can be found in used bookstores on the Islands and online.

Good Housekeeping Ultimate Grilling Cookbook: 250 Sizzling Recipes by Susan Westmoreland
This comprehensive cookbook came out in 2018 and makes grilling accessible for everyone, from first-timers to the seasoned pro looking for a new recipe to tweak. It provides 250 tasty grilling recipes with valuable tips, like the kind your grandma imparts, such as how to peel ginger and not waste any.

Hari Kojima's Local-Style Favorites by Hari Kojima
Hari Kojima was host of *Let's Go Fishing*, a popular TV show here in Hawaiʻi, teaching generations of viewers how to catch, cut, and cook fish. This 1987 book is out of print, but copies occasionally show up for sale online. Here on Oʻahu there is at least one copy circulating in the library and dozens in pantries.

The Hawaiʻi Tailgate Cookbook: Grilling Recipes from Top Island Chefs by Jo McGarry
Designed around tailgating at Aloha Stadium, each recipe is tailored for sharing. Some of Hawaiʻi's leading chefs, including Roy Yamaguchi, Alan Wong, Russel Siu, and Colin Nishida, share their best grill recipes in an easy-to-follow format. Published in 2004, copies can be found online.

How to Grill Everything: Simple Recipes for Great Flame-Cooked Food by Mark Bittman
If you're enthusiastic about grilling, Mark Bittman's 2018 book is a must-have. He literally knows how to grill everything and includes around one thousand recipes in this book.

A Hundred Years of Island Cooking: A Collection of Recipes from Hawaiian Electric Company edited by Pat Rea and Regina Ting
This 1991 cookbook is now out of print, but if you come across a copy at the library or at a friend's parents' house, you have found a treasure.

Island Flavors: Favorite Recipes of the Historic Hawaiʻi Foundation
This gem of a book was published in 1996 and nowadays is only found in family cookbook collections and the library.

Kau Kau: Cuisine and Culture in the Hawaiian Islands by Arnold Hiura
Celebrating its 10th anniversary with a beautiful 2020 reprint, this book chronicles the history of food on the Islands. Featuring photographs that date back into the last century and recipes that Hawai'i is known for, whether it rests on your coffee table or in your kitchen it is a conversation starter.

Let's Go Fishing Cookbook: Favorite Seafood Recipes from the Islands of Hawai'i and Beyond by Ben Wong
Published in 2011 and occasionally available online, this book's seafood recipes are second to none.

Pidgin to Da Max by Douglas Simonson (PEPPO), in collaboration with Ken Sakata and Pat Sasaki
My dad bought this illustrated pidgin dictionary when it came out in 1981 and I memorized every single cartoon. The Creole language that was born of Hawai'i's melting pot of cultures is chronicled with humor and insight. If you're not sure what someone is saying in pidgin, this book explains it.

Pupus to Da Max by Pat Sasaki, Douglas Simonson, and Ken Sakata
Published in 1986 by Bess Press, who gave us *Pidgin to Da Max*, this book is the self-proclaimed "All-Purpose Illustrated Guide to the Food of Hawaii." It's a dictionary and a recipe book combined, so you can make loco moco, haupia, and even malasadas at home.

CONVERSIONS

VOLUME

US	US EQUIVALENT	METRIC
1 tablespoon (3 teaspoons)	½ fluid ounce	15 milliliters
¼ cup	2 fluid ounces	60 milliliters
⅓ cup	3 fluid ounces	80 milliliters
½ cup	4 fluid ounces	120 milliliters
⅔ cup	5 fluid ounces	160 milliliters
¾ cup	6 fluid ounces	180 milliliters
1 cup	8 fluid ounces	240 milliliters
2 cups	16 fluid ounces	480 milliliters

WEIGHT

US	METRIC
½ ounce	15 grams
1 ounce	30 grams
2 ounces	60 grams
¼ pound	115 grams
⅓ pound	150 grams
½ pound	225 grams
¾ pound	340 grams
1 pound	450 grams

TEMPERATURE

FAHRENHEIT (°F)	CELSIUS (°C)
200°F	95°C
220°F	105°C
240°F	115°C
260°F	125°C
280°F	140°C
300°F	150°C
325°F	165°C
350°F	175°C
375°F	190°C
400°F	200°C
425°F	220°C
450°F	230°C

ACKNOWLEDGMENTS

I would like to first and foremost thank my husband, Dan Lowrie, who taught me how to light a grill, multiple times. A big mahalo to our keiki, Bea and Ian, who were patient as I grilled outside their bedrooms and stored many marinated meats in the fridge, making cheese sticks hard to find.

Mahalo to my mom, Lily Robillard, for her constant encouragement and enthusiasm and for saying, "If it doesn't work out, you're at least learning some new recipes." Mahalo to my extended 'ohana for believing in my ability to see this through.

To my grandmother, Dora Gin, for sharing her tried and true recipes, including the hot dog bacon and onion topping in this book. She taught me the best things are often the easiest to make, and if they don't come out the first time, try again.

Mahalo to friends and family here in the Islands and on the mainland for sharing their recipes, cookbooks, and tips. Mahalo to Monica Toguchi Ryan and Highway Inn for the loan of dishes and chafers, and to Masa Hawai'i for parking-lot delivery of their locally made fresh tortillas.

Thank you to the Hawai'i State Public Library system, in particular the Kailua branch. Mahalo to Morning Brew, Kailua, where the majority of this cookbook was written and organized, where the brisk AC kept me focused, and where Cheryl Resor and I pieced together conversations from just a few sentences at a time.

If Traci Morinaga had not introduced me to Dawn Sakamoto Paiva, this book would not be beautiful (or exist). Thank you, Dawn, for embarking on this collaboration with me. And mahalo to Derek, Dawn's husband, an essential taste tester and voice of reason on those days when we had been grilling for hours and couldn't quite tell if we were crazy to drizzle teriyaki sauce on grilled lettuce.

Mahalo to Tess Bevernage and Thomas Robillard, my brother, from Hānai Family Table, who shared both their delicious teriyaki recipes and their enthusiasm for bringing people together over 'ono food. To my brother Terry, for his support, consistent love of chicken teriyaki, and keeping me company on all those flights we took back and forth from the Islands to California in the '80s and '90s.

It takes a neighborhood to write a cookbook. Peggy and Keith Zeilinger shared a whole salmon they received from a friend of a friend who had returned from an Alaskan fishing trip with it. The

Zeilingers also contributed breadfruit, bananas, and some essential wine and beer to the creation of this book. Mahalo to our neighbor Betty Donaldson for gifting guava puree and fresh guavas from her yard and introducing me to *Fruits of Hawaii*. Mahalo to Jackie Boland and Heidi Picker for loaning their beautiful platters, for their enthusiasm, and for taste-testing many of the recipes found here with their families.

And mahalo to all the people of Hawai'i for making food that welcomes friends and family, brings people together, and creates opportunities to talk story so we can build community in our world.

ABOUT THE AUTHOR

Adrienne Robillard is a writer and an English lecturer in the early college program at Windward Community College in Kāneʻohe, Hawaiʻi. She grew up in Kailua, Hawaiʻi, and Fresno, California. After college she worked in San Francisco as a technology editor by day and fronted indie-rock bands by night, opening for The Decemberists and Arcade Fire in the US and playing shows in deconsecrated churches and underground clubs in the UK and Europe.

She lives with her husband and their two children in Kailua on Oʻahu. A member of the Hawaiian Islands Chapter of the Society of Children's Book Writers and Illustrators, she is also a contributing writer to *Hawaii Business*. Her short story "24-Hour Grocery" was published in the San Francisco zine *Spunk* before the internet exploded. In the summer of 2017 she participated in the Tin House Summer Workshop for a novel-in-progress. Her essay "Try Wait" was published in the March 2018 "America" issue of the *We'll Never Have Paris* zine.

ABOUT THE PHOTOGRAPHER

Dawn Sakamoto Paiva has two decades of experience in the book and magazine publishing industries. She has worked on numerous award-winning cookbooks with prominent Hawaiʻi chefs and has a passion for food and drink. In 2014, she started her own business, Put It On My Plate, which offers communications, marketing and event coordination services, photography, writing, and editing, and specializes in working with chefs, restaurants, bars, and food-related businesses.

Paiva was born and raised in Windward Oʻahu, Hawaiʻi, is a graduate of ʻIolani high school, and earned her degree in English from Kenyon College in Ohio. She is a member of Les Dames d'Escoffier, Hawaiʻi Chapter, and maintains (off and on!) a blog, *Sugar + Shake*, where she chronicles her adventures in food, drink, and, sometimes, travel.

Printed in the USA
CPSIA information can be obtained
at www.ICGtesting.com
CBHW062156170624
10247CB00003B/17